Enjoy your Reading.

Copyright © Jessie Larman 2025

Published by: Carnarvon Art Studio 2025

All rights reserved. This book is copyright. Apart from any fair dealing for the purpose of private study, research, criticism or review, as permitted under the Copyright Act, no part of this book may be reproduced or transmitted in any form or by any means, electronic or mechanical, including photocopying, recording or by any information storage and retrieval systems without written permission from the publisher. Enquiries should be made to the publisher.

National Library of Australia

A catalogue record for this book is available from the National Library of Australia

ISBN: 978-1-7640965-0-8 (paperback)
ISBN: 978-1-7640965-1-5 (ebook)
Distributed in Australia and Overseas by Ingram Content Group

I hope you enjoy some of the Verses and Poems
in this book as much as I have enjoyed writing them.
Some are funny some are serious,
some are a bit odd but it all lends to the tapestry of life,
a different kind of reading.
They are not in any order so just open anywhere
to read something.

Maybe share with a friend.

*****

My Father.....

My Father - Earnest George Wyatt (my Dad) started to teach me Poetry when I was quite young. In the Winter we used to sit close together in the front room by the fire. Looking into the coal burning in the fireplace. Dad used to sing or play his mouth organ. Then we would just sit quietly and watch the redness of the coal burn.

Dad was demobbed from the Army when I was 8yrs old (Second World War) with Shell Shock. He was in the trenches in France with the French, English and Irish Solders etc;

So growing up I learnt to sing the lovely Irish songs that he learnt side by side with the Solders in the trenches'. I only remember the first couple of lines of the Poem we were inventing that night sitting by the fire. The Fireplace had a nice Mantle piece with Mum's ornament's on. (Mum never joined in with our singing and poetry)

Here is the start of the Poem that I remember and how he was trying to teach me. Looking at the Clock on the Mantelpiece he said 'think what we can write about the Clock?' So this is what we came up with...

The Clock on the Mantelpiece has a round face. It has two hands that never keep pace.

He was teaching me how to Rhyme different words. Dad was a loving Father and was only 52years old when he died.

Cont'd.......

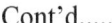

Cont'd.....

Here is a bit more about him... He used to tend his garden and allotment with Vegetables, Flowers and Fruit, which he loved to enter in the Local Competitions.

Chrysanthemum's and Dahlias (Flowers) were his favourite's.

One year the Chrysanth's grew heads as big as dinner plates, he was so proud of them growing in rows in our back garden amongst the Potatoes, Cabbages, Tomatoes, Runner Beans, Blackcurrants, Red currents, Gooseberries etc., Well, my young brother thought he would be helpful and cut all the heads off of the Prize Flowers. Poor Dad was horrified as they were just ready for the Exhibition and Competition. Each year he won awards for Flowers, Blackcurrants and other produce. He let my sister and I have a small piece of garden about a meter square for us to grow whatever we would like, so we learnt at an early age what to do.

We had Chickens at the bottom of the garden mostly for eggs and to eat.

They were well fed as Dad used to cook for them over a little gas stove in the shed..... All the peelings from the vegetables were cooked in water and oats with chicken meal added. - Sometimes I sat in there to help and we tasted the cooked meal to see if it was good enough for the Chickens!

Cont'd......

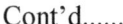

Cont'd......

"Henrietta" laid an enormous Egg as big as a Duck Egg - she was the favourite and we could hold her and stroke her soft brown feathers.
But the day came for her to be our Sunday dinner.
With all of us children sitting around the table waiting for our lovely Chicken Dinner - as Mum brought out the veggies and batter puddings, ...
Dad suddenly said - when he was about to carve the beautiful Roast Chicken "Poor Henrietta" ... all went quiet and approx. six pairs of little eyes had tears in them and would not eat Henrietta.

Will stop writing about my Father now and get on with the Poetry and Verses Book.
Dad would have been so proud to know that he had helped regarding my Poems and Verses.
We were a very poor family and had no books at home apart from our School books. So Dad would have also liked to have known that I have become an Author and an Artist.

I hope you enjoy some of my writings
in this book.

Jessie.

*****

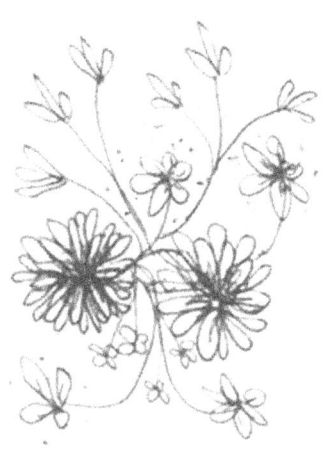

So - open a page don't be shy,

laugh or cry, it doesn't matter.

This is our world of Poem's and Verses.

Open the Book and have a Look.

Enjoy what is written on the Page's.

No need to hurry - take your time.

It could be lovely day.

*****

<u>Beauty of a Rose</u>

The beauty of a Rose
is beyond compare.
The petals so soft
as they take in the air.
The colours so subtle
as well as bright and strong.
The perfume out passes
even our loveliest song.
The Rose has thorns
on the stems and the stalks.
The thorns are protection
from predators walks.
So touch a petal
smell the Rose.
The perfume will be
wonderful to your nose.
Find time, look
at its beauty it is so timeless.
Be refreshed with it's perfume,
it's softness it's loveliness.
Maybe it's time to put
a Rose in your home,
to look at each day
and not feel alone.

Jessie 23rd. Jan. 2013

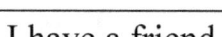

I have a friend.

I have a friend -
who shall be nameless.
He lives within my heart.
Every day is a new day
to think of him,
even though we are apart.
Does he even know
that I care for him.
Really does it matter
that I care?
Well - yes it does,
as it is good to have a friend.
Not an imaginary one,
just a real friend - even far away.
How far away you may well ask?
Distance does not matter
when he lives
within my heart.

***

Tall and Straight.

I was tall and straight and lovely and slim.
But now I am bent and very thin.
But my memory is good and I can look back to see,
of the young Person I used to be.
Now I am old and they say I am frail.
But on the inside I feel much like I used to be.
My body won't do the things now that I want it to do.
So sometimes I just sit and remember the things I did do!
What a wonderful life I have lived here on this Planet Earth.
Since the beginning of my Birth.

Day by Day, Year by Year time has flown and here I am now in the time of my -
Twilight Years.

*****

Jessie 19th. March 2025. Thursday.

Dear Founder, of the Falling Down Society.

We understand that **Falling Down** requires a **Great Art** i.e.

(1) **Gracefully being Airborne** before coming into contact with Terra firma (earth for those uninitiated), or maybe coming into contact with a Pavement, Road or Grassland.

(2) **Falling down Stairs** - even Greater Grace & Dexterity is required - for instance should one fall head first, bottom sliding down stairs or feet first?
That is the Question!

(3) **Falling over a cliff** would most likely be **Fatal**, Grace, Dexterity etc., would not help - So just go for it!

(4) **When you find yourself tripping** - usual thing is to go Upward i.e. being Airborne before landing with bodily force - sometimes hands stretched out and sliding forward to help stop the impact of landing! Sometimes, hands get Skin Shredded, Knees take a Knock and get Grazed.
Other body parts are not too keen to be treated like this, so they respond by Hurting, Aching, Dislocating or - **Bits Falling Off!**

Cont'd.....

Cont'd.....

As Founder of the Society,
>are you doing your U<u>tmost</u> to keep in fashion with your Society Members by demonstrating the Art of Falling?

i.e. By Gracefully Flying Up, Down, or Rolling Around, are you able to get to the sitting up position before standing upright again.

>Are you not taking too much gravel with you if knees come in contact with the roadside.

You need to be a good example incase your Members of the Society are on Watch Duty!!!?

****

A Deadly Strain of Chicken.

A deadly strain of Chickens
Has been produced in Carnarvon
Laying Atomic like Yolks
They are Round and Yellow.
After being in the Microwave
In milk for Scrambled Egg
(which had not been blended)
On the touch of a Fork Prong
(when taken out of the Microwave)
Did Explode in all Directions
Causing Havoc to Person & Draining Board.
Kitchen Cupboards, Wall & Window.
The Exploding Yolk Erupted
With an Almighty BANG
And covered a Wide Area
With YELLOW BITS.
These Chickens must be
Severely dealt with - maybe fed
With a Softer Layers Mash. !
Not the usual hard Pellets. !!!

Oh! What a YOLK.

………………………….

Jessie……August 2007.

"Pansy Flower"

Hello, I am a Pansy Flower, with a face upon my Petals.

My face is full of colour - Purple, Red and Yellow.
You can see my face if you look quite closely.
My face looks to the sky.
Although I am beautiful I am really quite shy.
I hide among the taller plants, they are so high and lofty.
But I don't mind a bit, because I'll never - ever be lonely.
We usually grow in clusters you see,
us dearest little 'Pansies'.
Children love to peer at us, they wonder if we can see them!
Yes of course we can.
We see the Sun, we feel the breeze, the lovely refreshing rain.
We love to grow in our little clumps and we cheer you up if you feel down in the dumps.
I have no arms or legs you know but I have good strong leggy roots.
So grow me in your garden beds or put me in a pot.
Please put me somewhere it is really not too hot.

> Remember I am your little Pansy friend
> with a beautiful friendly face.

*****

THE POD   (from my Sister Jill)

My Sister sent a Seed Pod, an enormous thing it was.
I planted it with loving care
and watched and watched and watched.
But nothing ever happened until the post arrived.
"Dig it up" she said, I was most surprised.
It was all brown and wrinkly and very shriveled too,
"You mustn't plant it whole" she said, that must never do.
I cut it up and looked inside, my goodness what a sight.
T'was green and brown and mangy,
it gave me quite a fright.

I did as I was told, I hope I've done it right.
It's lying in it's little bed, it's really tucked up tight.
So in a month or two I'm sure, the Pod will start to sprout.
I hope it doesn't grow to big, as the greenhouse is quite small.
About my height would be just right, a nice size for a tree.
Then I could look it in the eye,
for I'm only 5'3.

*****

To Jessie from Jill.
Thought you would like this little ditty.

Posted to me 23rd. August 1991

At the Market Place.

I see them growing older, the ones I love, the ones I care about. Those strangers in the market place. The older ones I mean. I never used to notice the tired faces, some racked with pain trying to live life, hoping to feel young again.
Young people pushing prams with babies in them.
Toddlers touching, tasting new things on the market stalls.
Friends and neighbours meeting, stopping to chat and share their news. Sometimes sad, sometimes glad.

At our homes we rarely meet, it's different to see them in the street. In between the Market stalls, tourists meander here and there. Many years sometimes go by before we meet a strangers eye, only to find that face now old was once a beauty to behold.
Suddenly I realize, yes I know that face, goodness, gracious how they've changed. But they, looking at us think must the same. We recognize each other and think what a shame that age has caught up with us.
We hug and kiss and Oh! What bliss to find our friend in these twilight years.

I sit and watch as people go by, they don't all come to the market to buy, mainly just to look and fellowship amongst the other tourists and our township people.
Some come to browse at local Authors books, some to buy Hot-dogs, doughnuts, exotic food stuffs, ice creams and plants or fresh foods.

Cont'd....

Cont'd....

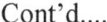

Some children are having their faces painted, a foot massage is the way to go for some of the adults. While others peruse the jewelry stalls, the clothes and other things.

Pregnant Mums and dogs on leads all help to make the market live.

Children watch a puppet show, they too will grow old like one of us here and maybe sit and watch the same as me.

Gophers are the way to go now and weave in-between the crowd of shoppers.

I sit at my stall with my books for sale, watching the world go by.

I have my coffee and a comfortable chair, a dear friend to sit with and also to share the Courtyard Market morning. This is my Social morning at the Courtyard Crafts.

This is a saga that never ends, of babies, toddlers and teens, Mums and Dads, Nanna's and Granddads, Uncles and Aunts, it's a never ending cycle of life!

*****

What is more Precious to you?

What is more precious to you
To have a new boat, caravan,
or to have a new baby?
To give life to a new human being is a great
privilege to watch them grow, to love and console,
to feed and clothe them.
What joy in your older years to have their love and
support.
The caravan and boat will rust and decay
but your family can be there for you each day.
Even into old age they can be a blessing to you.
Then what memories you will treasure,
of your care and love for them.
So - young people please don't abort the wonderful
life that is given.
Bring to birth another beautiful little soul and nurture
it with love.
Enjoy every moment if you can.
Because God may have a wonderful plan
for the new little baby about to be born.
The more love you give the more you receive.
Don't be waylaid with money or greed.
The boat, caravan or baby what shall it be?
What Blessings I have now that I am older, even
eleven Grandchildren I've held on my shoulder.

*****

Jessie 27th. Feb. 2008.

Shopping in our Supermarket.!

Well I couldn't reach the Cooking Margarine.
Try as I may it was way out of reach.
On the top shelf right at the back, the one that I like!
Shoppers had reached and brought the others
near the front from off that top shelf.
I was thinking - No, I had better not stand on the
lower Deli Cheese and Butter shelf to reach up -
When along came a friend, another older lady
like myself and she said "What you doing there"
I told her and she said "don't worry gal I'll get it for
you" "How can you" I asked "you are even shorter
than me"
"Well I've got a secret weapon" she replied,
waving her long half stalk of Celery in front of me.
So she leapt up with the Celery to dislodge the
Margarine which pushed it out of sight, further back.
Laughing, waving the half stalk of Celery she poised
for another go. This time lodging another brand off
to tumble below.
Laughing like giggling girls holding on to our shopping trollies for support, a taller young woman asked
if were alright and could she help?
"No" she said I don't need the Stick of Celery
to reach the Margarine. Then she kindly retrieved it
for us. Well, we have to laugh sometimes at these
things to do our best as pensioners to reach the
unreachable.
Even growing shorter - we still need to eat !!!!

*****

Jessie. June 2008.

A Resume .... for a friend re: House Cleaning.
<u>To Whom it may Concern!</u>

What can I say?
Well,- punctuality is very good give or take a few minutes here & there.
Yes - extension lead is collected from our shed after garbage bin, if not already brought in is trundled up the drive way.
She looks to see if cats have ben fed. Saunters down the back steps and takes up position, standing, by the kitchen sink, while waiting for me to make her favourite Cuppa.
I have my breakfast while the one who is helping me - talks to me and drinks her Cuppa.
No housework yet as <u>Social Time Takes priority.</u>
In between mouthfuls of breakfast, I sometimes can get a word in - we take turns catching up on worldly events!
Then off she goes to vacuum the Studio but wait! Something we forgot to tell each other - so vacuum off for a while. (Vacuum Cleaner often has a rest)
After catching up on extra news, we each start our cleaning schedule. But Wait - by now it is just about time for Morning Tea.....Time for another Cuppa.
We do not stop work for this as TIME is now pressing on and getting away from us. We quickly speed up now with our chores to finish with a flourish by lunchtime.
To Whom it may concern she is an excellent helper.

*****

Reference - Jessie. December 2008

I Just Remembered

I just remembered, did I forget to do that
or - did I do it and forget that I did it?
I forget now but if I do it now and
I have already done it, that means that I
would have done it twice.
Best if I don't do it now.
I may not have done it at all
if I didn't do it in the first place.
What a dilemma, why did I just think that
I hadn't done it, then think that maybe I had.
Well, I remember thinking that I should
but I wonder if I did.
The best thing is to go and look I suppose -
- now what was it that I think I forgot to do.
I can't remember now,
best to have a Cuppa and think about it later.

*****

When is a Baby not a Baby ?

When is a Baby not a Baby ?
When is a child not a child?
When is a teenager not a teenager?
When is a teenager an adult, an adult a parent?
An adult can become a Mother.
Also an adult can become a Father.
The Mother later becomes a Grandmother.
A Father likewise becomes a Grandfather.
After this they can become Great Grandfather
and Great Grandmother.
They can become G.G. Grandparents but
not often do they live that long.
Then they are gone and the Cycle keeps on keeping
on. So there we are - a Baby, a Child, a teenager,
then an Adult. Life continues in a never ending
circle, with all these stages of life.
While on this Earth we have a Destiny.
Each one is different, each individual, is
different in colour, creed and body.
Be yourself - the way you were made, as a Special
Baby, Child, Teenager and Adult.
So where are you at now? Enjoy your life if you
can, just where you are now in this time of life.
Soon it will be gone and the next Stage of life will
be there.
You do not see the transgression from one stage to
the next. It just happens without our help and we are
there.

*****

Jessie 14th. Oct. 2014. Tuesday

Laughter & Joy

Laughter and Joy are from The Lord.
So let us embrace today.
Open your heart let the Joy in.
It's a pity to give into that sin.
There can be no peace if we continue to sin
because the heart cannot let the Joy come in.

What is Life without Laughter and Joy?
Even for a moment during the day relax and let go
of the sins that you know.
Joy will begin in that moment of time.

Open your heart to make a fresh start and walk in
confidence, being unafraid to show your Joyful heart.

When you do that even Laughter can start.
Just a little giggle is all that it needs
for real laughter and Joy to begin.

*****

Jessie. 23rd. Jan. 2013

Chance

So how can I write anything or something about Chance? Chances are it may not work but then chances are it will.

Well then, what is chance? It really often means taking a risk. Why would I want to take a risk if I thought that by chance it would not work.

Oh! I took a chance when I was young, that really was a risk to be tempted by a kiss. All common sense flies away in the moment of passion. Because a chance like that may never come again - and it didn't!

We look a chance not to declare our love, that was a risk, because how can you hide the joy, the feeling so sublime -well, chances are you can't, can you?

People notice that you have a glow about you, a peace about you, a secret looking smile - But sometimes that love fades away and you cannot understand why.

However I believe it is better to have loved and lost than never to have loved at all.

Chance then was a fine thing, something to remember for ever. The wonderful kiss, the warm embrace will live in my heart forever.

What were the chances that we should meet again?

Never I would say but chance is an odd thing.

So by chance years later in a room full of people, most of whom I did not know, while I was looking around, just by chance our eyes met.

Over the years our bodies, our looks had altered but those eyes, I was sure they were his. He looked older of course after thirty years of us being apart. Yes, I could see that he had put on some weight but not much, just enough to make him look even more handsome than he was as a twenty year old. His hair had a touch of grey making him look very distinguished and desirable.

Cont'd ....

As for myself well....I was not that slim young thing anymore but still had quite a decent figure with a good healthy head of hair (involving a bit of colour tint of course) not enough to notice though!

So, I was not sure what to do, standing there feeling a bit overwhelmed with the situation. Then as we looked at each other across the room full of party goers who were there to celebrate someone's birthday - suddenly we saw!

What did we see? Our loving eyes just looking deep into each others souls. Chance then was a fine thing!

We took a chance and walked across that room holding each other with our eyes. Then came the embrace - it was as if we had never been apart.

Years fell away and we felt like the young lovers that we first were. Just by chance it seemed at that encounter, that special time, we were both free to renew our love our wonderful friendship that we had so many years ago.

Party goers watched as we took to the floor for the next dance - it seemed that we just melted into each others arms. To dance with the love of your life is so special, no words can describe the feeling.

So chance can be a wonderful thing in so many ways.

To find my first love once more was a chance that I would not have wanted to miss. So then what is Chance - it is a coming together of many things, some good, some not so good. But a second chance can be wonderful.

We decided to take another Chance of beginning again to recapture the rapture of those early years. And we did it even in our golden days. Days of sunsets and evening glows - we can sit in oneness in the gratefulness of having this marvelous chance of belonging to each

other. Nothing nor no-one can shatter our peace or joy as we relive our long ago love.

If we have a Chance to take a Chance, then why not take a Chance if you feel that is the right thing for you to do.

Where Am I

I sit here surrounded by beautiful Art.
Music is playing, so that plays a part.
What is this in this quiet room here?
Apart from the sound of the melodies coming
from the cheap little music cassette player,
nothing is moving not even a hair, not a breeze
or the Sun shining into the room.
Fluorescent light is not the same as bright sunlight or sunshine.
I can hear the Birds chirping outside and the
vehicles driving up and down the street.
Yes, this is an Art Gallery with Beautiful Art -
Paintings, some bold and bright, others filled with
light and love.
Some full of colour, some black & white.
It is a privilege to sit among them, to look and see
some of Gods Creation depicted in colourful hues.
The vast Outback, some tiny flowers, Birds and Beasts.
One White Tiger looking out from the canvas,
a Giraffe Silhouette on another, Palm Trees and Sunsets.
All just waiting for new owners to come for them.
What will it be that you choose to live with in your
home as a family heirloom?
What will others think of your choice?
However, I hope that you receive great pleasure
from your own special Art that you choose.

Jessie July 2013

Should I write on this Page?

Shall I write on this Page?
If so what should I write?
The day is here, the night has gone, it is a new day today!
All over the World people are waking, the slumber is being washed from their eyes.
Children are waking, wanting to be cared for.
Grandparents, also the elderly people are slower to waken from their nights sleep.
So what shall I write? It is a New Day.
This is a new Page of life that has not been lived before.
All our yesterdays are gone blown away like the wind.
Today will have cares of it's own but by nighttime the day will be gone once more.
Night will come - when the day is ended.
Sleep will come to refresh and renew us.
Then, when we awake a New Day will have Dawned.
Ready for us to write a New Page of our Life.
So, what shall I write on this Page, this New Day of my Life?
I pray that I will be thankful to write for the Blessings I have - and have had on the past pages of my life.
Also for the Blessings that are to come.
So, that is what I should write!
        What do you think?
*****

Jessie April 2018.

Contentment

Contentment is a funny word!
What does it actually mean?
Does it mean to live at peace with myself and others.
Or to stay calm in the midst of strife?
No, it doesn't mean to stay calm in days of strife.
It really means - I think to be at one with myself.
(I mean at peace with myself)
To be glad of who I am to be thankful of what and
where I am. When we are content in all circumstances
we can stop rushing around just to please others.
We can take time to sit and think. Contentment is a
feeling that we need to have, so that we do not keep
striving for things. If we are rich or poor - we can be
content with what we have or wherever we are.
The storms of life will come to us all at some stage of
our life. But we must try to overcome and to count our
Blessings each and every day.
Each day will be different from the next, remember
we have to live through each day. So if we try to have
Peace in our heart, that is a really good start - to try to
be content. Contentment is lovely, we need have no
fear. Because peace in our hearts cancels all fear.
Each day is a New Day to be thankful.
Maybe when we show someone we care, that helps
us to be content in ourselves when we feel we have
talked or helped someone. Like a baby that is well fed
and loved it smiles with Contentment on it's face.

So Contentment can show too on our face.

*****

Jessie. 1st. October. 2019. Tuesday.

<u>The Day is Here.....</u>

The day is here a new day in our lives.
The daylight is precious the night has gone.
Morning has come the day has begun.
What shall we do with the day that is new?
Let us rejoice in the light that is here.
Night has gone so we now have no fear.
Some are afraid of the dark but morning has come.
Maybe hear the Lark or the Dog bark?
Look outside, open your eyes the new day has dawned.
A whole New Day to laugh & play to work or to shirk.
Whatever you feel - the day is ours, so we can begin with a smile or a sigh.
To be able to get up is a blessing let us not waste today.
There is a lot to do -
Maybe meet and greet our family and friends.
Go for a walk, a ride or just sit and meditate a while.

The day is here
a new day in our lives
has just begun.

*****

Jessie 30th. September 2020 Wednesday.

North West State of Western Australia.

North West State of Western Australia, with your heat and vast expanse of land. How I adore you, you wonderful place, staring at me with your changing face.

You look so bleak and bare in places, with salt bush covering thousands of acres. Sheep walking for hundreds of miles covered in sand with red earth dust over once white fleece. Red dust clinging to them and to everything - blown by the wind from your desert-like landscape.

Hot winds creating 'Willy-Willies' sometimes taking dust up into the air hundreds of metres, swirling it around like great whirl-winds collecting debris on the way depositing it further along as the 'Willy-Willy' dissipates into nothingness.

They are so force-full that you could be sucked up and swirled around if ever you dared to challenge one.

That's all in the Dry Season but in the Wet - you have a different Face,

you are a different being, with vast acres.

Millions of acres of wild flowers - yellow maybe, for miles and miles?

Changing to purple or maybe blue? Then further on beautiful pink.

Oh! You are a wonderful sight, the vast North West.

Cont'd.....

Your wild life is just as exotic. Kangaroo's hopping and Emu's running, what a sight to see, all Gods creatures roaming free.
The Fox and the Dingo admitted are pests, like-wise the Rabbits. But to watch them at play is a privileged sight you must agree.
So one day soon come with me - watch the Galah's and White Cockatoo's. Budgerigar in their hundreds as well. The lovely green Parrots and the bird life in full, complete the vast canvas that was given for all.

You cannot but Love the North West of our State.
- So, come on -
Give it a go - good on you mate!
……………………………………

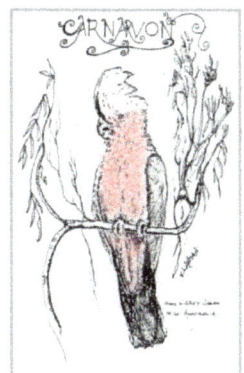

A Runner Bean

I am a Bean -
the Greenest Bean you have ever seen.
I am long and thin but I have a secret within.
I grow on a Vine with my other Green Brothers.
We all look the same hanging down from the Vine.
We came from a flower that gave us our birth.
We are Special you know to grow on this Earth.
Our Secret within is - a Seed that can be saved and dried for another Green Bean to grow.
You can pick me and eat me fresh from the vine
Or cook me and eat me I am Slender and Beautiful .... and just Divine!

*****

Jessie. 1st. September 2024.

Muffin Tops

The day of reckoning comes -
Sunday after morning Service, before Morning Tea,
just incase - that piece of cake, biscuit or scone
may put on the extra Stone.
So in we went prepared to weigh. Sue prepared a
Graph so we would not stray from eating healthy
food. Well, she had brought along her Scales, for us
to stand upon.
We looked in humorous horror at the white mostly
Rusty thing, straight from the paddock or horses
yard covered in bits of Stuff & Brown from Rust.
We thought we should keep our shoes on before
standing on the Scales then extract a bit of weight, to
compensate.
Well, they did not ring true, the marker hovered
around on the weight dial. Our Muffin Tops seemed
very weighty, so our Graphs were very High.
Someone suggested New Scales we should buy.
Now we have some Posh new Scales.
You have to step on, then off, then on again so they
can register your weight. Our Graphs have gone
down a bit now and our <u>Figures</u> are getting <u>Slight.</u>
<u>Muffin Tops </u>are Rare now in our Congregation.
At first I did not know what a Muffin Top was or
that they even existed.
Apparently they used to be called - Spare Tyres.

(Just above your waist incase you did not know)
*****

Jessie 28th. October 2010.

Today is Ours to Live

These are the days of our lives - today, tomorrow, yesterday. What are we doing with them?
Where are we now, where have we been, where will we go?
Some have been to the depths of despair.
Some to the heights of glory.
Today is a new day, a time to begin.
Start with a clean sheet at the beginning of the morning.
Just as a page is in a book or a canvas for painting, today will hold the picture that we are painting with our life.
The mornings can start with a Prayer or a curse.
The day will progress unfolding as a flower,
like petals unfolding until the flower is in full bloom.
So lets start the day with a prayer and blow away the gloom.
Let us get up from our bed try to smile and rejoice.
Remember God has given us a voice.
Use it bless those we see today.
Tell them you love them enrich their day.
We shall be blessed when we live this way.

Today is ours to live.

*****

Jessie. June 2010

- Piggy's Home -

It is so lovely here, so warm and lush to nuzzle in the damp dark earth under each tree, bush and grass.
There is a muddy large swampy area just to the left of the gate. In it I can wallow, turn, sit and squirm to my hearts content. No one to bother me, no one to see just beautiful squashy mud and me.
Oh! the Bliss, the wonderful Bliss.
To wallow like this is better than that old Hogs kiss.
I am so proud of my beautiful body, Pink with dark black patches and spots. My lovely Pot Belly is beautiful to behold and I have the cutest curly tail that goes around at the back end of me.
Well, you should see my piglet eyes my pointy ears and dainty trotters. Oh! I am so beautiful, my Mistress tells me this sometimes - even with a kiss.
She says that she won't mention that word BACON in my presence - I don't know what she means as she whispers it to her friends.
Yes, they come to see me and gaze on my loveliness.
My Mistress is so proud of me. She bathes me, hoses me down, dries me with a soft, so soft towel, tucks me under her arm and takes me into her house. I am put onto my special bed, to watch their television.
I lay and look in wonder at the pictures on the screen.
Beautiful tidbits the family feed me from their own dinner before my Mistress takes me back to my Sty.
It's lovely indoors but I much prefer my Pig Sty - it is my home, my very own. I can snuffle around in it as much as I please. My home has big shady trees, with lots of tall grass but the mud puddle, swampy area is the best place of all. I could lay in that for ever and ever and ever.
I am so, so blessed with such a beautiful home.

*****

Written by me Jessie. (For a Pet Pig Owner).

Oink ! Oink !

Are you Beautiful ?

Beauty is not just in the eye of the beholder
(that means the one who is looking at you)!
Let them know that beauty is within you.
Tell yourself that Beauty is loveliness.
Beauty will show on your face if you have peace in
your heart.
You may not be good looking, intelligent or smart
but beauty can be on your face by the look of the
contentment that is in your heart.
Superficial beauty of make-up and paint on the face
and body will be gone.
But the beauty of Grace, Contentment and Peace,
can be everlasting in your soul, in your heart, in
your being, in your understanding.
Yes beauty is fleeting but Love in your heart can
flow out to others if only you can let it flow to
bless others that come before you each day.
Let them know that you care for them, talk to them,
help them.
Then beauty will shine from you and it will not
be Fleeting.

*****

Jessie. April 2018

The Window.

Have you looked out of the Window today?
Have you opened the Curtains and Blinds?
What do you see from your Window today?
Look out at the Sky through the Window Pane.
Is it blue or is it grey - is it dark or is it light?
Much depends on how you feel when you look.
If the sky is Grey you may feel sad.
But if it is blue then you can feel glad.
Each day is different from the day before
so look out first before opening your door.
Where will you go, what will you do
with the new day you have been given?
So get up and get ready to face the day,
there are lots of things you can do and say.
Have a nice breakfast what ever the weather.
Try not to rush if you have time have a Cuppa.
A nice breakfast and drink is a good way to start.
This day only comes once so give it a chance.

*****
Jessie. 5th. November.
Thursday 2020

A Roving Eye.

I have a roving eye, I look to and fro.
Up and down and roundabout.
Who or what do I see?
Mainly I scan the Heavens.
I see small stars, large stars, Planets galore.
The Milky way is a pleasure to behold.
Saturn, Mercury, Venice and Mars are just a few to
let you know what I behold with my Roving Eye.
I am the Satellite Dish standing proud upon a hill
in Carnarvon, North Western Australia.
My Roving Eye can move around to see the
Heavenly Galaxy.
I am so proud to be able to see -
The Glory of the Outer World of our Universe.
No naked eye can see what I see.
I even saw the first men landing on the moon.
What a privilege to be a Satellite Dish
Standing upright and alone on the Hill.

*****

Jessie. 22nd. March 2023

This is the Photo that I took to use for my Painting on the front cover of this book.

Along the Pathway

I walked down the Pathway and saw a flower.
It was morning time not the earliest hour.
The sun was out and the bloom was beautiful.
Petals so soft stretching up towards the sun.
Quite large Petals so soft and new, opening up for me and you.
Glorious orange and red in colour growing on the sturdy branches of the green leafed tree.
Down the Pathway it adds some colour - to brighten our day and to see the wonder, the wonder of creation afresh each day.
As I walk along the Pathway
Day by day.

*****

Jessie 10th. August 2023.

Beautiful Poinciana tree in blossom along my Driveway.

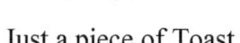

Just a piece of Toast.

A piece of Toast is what I am,
covered in Butter or covered in Jam.
Look at me - look at me, Round or Square.
I'm put in the toaster -it is hot in there.

Sometimes I come out with a lovely Tan colour
sometimes darker brown.
If they forget me I come out black.
When I come out looking very black, you can
have scrapped toast, it gives you a Charcoal flavour
and is real nice when you smother me with lovely
thick butter.

The brown colour when I am toasted are most
peoples favourite's, not too exciting but very nice to
eat.
When I come out of the toaster with a very
light tan that is special for the children to eat.

So there you are then, what more can I say,
accept that you can love me for Breakfast or Lunch.

Sometimes I am decorated with lovely things.
Shall I tell you what they are?
Here we are then look and see,
how you would really like to eat me?

Cont'd..........

1 - Egg on Toast for Breakfast is the way to go,
   Poached Fried, Boiled or Scrambled,
   what will it be?

Here are the Recipes:

If you have an Egg Poacher just follow instructions and cook your eggs.
Remember to Butter your Toast before putting the Poached Egg or Eggs on.

2 - Toast Talking: When you break the soft Yolk open it makes me feel all gooey when the Yolk rains all over me.

*****

Scrambled Egg.

2 - Eggs.
1cup - Milk, Pinch of Salt, Pepper to taste,
1 - Teaspoon Butter.
Put all in small Saucepan.
Beat with fork, bring gently to nearly boiling.
Stir till combined and cooked.

Ready to serve on the Toast.

*****

Bluebell Time
Colchester - England - Friday Woods.

We used to go Blue belling as children,
knee deep in beautiful bluebell flowers.
Wandering through the woods without a care.
Just lovely to be out in the fresh air.
We used to ride our bikes to the woods, leave them
at the edge of the trees and have fun running,
skipping, chasing each other between the trees and
Bluebells.
Never a thought of time or meal time, out all day to
laugh and play.
Always to pick a bunch of bluebells to take home
for Mum and Nanna.
Home before evening meal time, after cycling for
about half an hour to an hour, depending which way
we rode through the fields and country roads to go
home.
My Sister and I with a couple of friends riding
sometimes hands free, no hard hats then.
Feet off the pedals to sail down the hills.
We never really fell off, just used to ride along
sometimes singing odd songs with loud voices.
It's good to look back on some of these things.
Which then we took for granted with never a care
and never a fear.
        Just lovely childhood memories.

*****

Jessie. 19th. March. 2021. Friday.

Butterflies

Butterflies were flitting around as I walked along the garden path.
They were flitting all around me.
Pretty coloured wings they had that fluttered back and forth as flew around.
Such a lovely sight to behold.
So gently did they alight upon the flower blossoms.
Probably taking a small breath before taking off into the wind again.
So incredible to see the patterns on their wings.
Each Butterfly the same as the other.
Where did they come from and where will they go?
  Maybe it's not for us to know.

*****

Jessie. 5th. May 2024. Sunday.

Covid 19....Corona Virus

Thank you for the video, I know its just a game.
After the lockdown we will never be the same.
Most of us may be better and some of us may be worse.
But what on earth does it matter if we can talk like this on earth.
On a Video in our own house, in the kitchen or the lounge room, maybe in the bedroom or even in the bath.
What does it really matter?
On here we can have a laugh.
We can laugh or sing or any old thing!
Some people dance to peculiar tunes, they put their gyrating's on for all to see on the public Video T.V.
While behind closed doors forgetting, really, that we can all see.
What a wonderful world the Lockdown can be.
I think now I'll have a cup of tea.
      Wait a minute - is there more?
      No I'll just close the door.

*****

Jessie. 9th. July 2020.

Cyclone Steve

We thank you Lord that the Cyclone has Past.
Having reformed itself three times.
Named Steve it was determined to last.
Around the top of Australia it came.
Then started down the West Coast, hovering here and hovering there!
Regrouping itself as if it could boast of its mighty winds and power.

The eye was watching the path to take, as it moved with awesome strength.
It circled and spun more power to make.
Then on its way it carefully went.
However, we prayed that the eye would go past all communities along our coast.
We watched as it came moving to & fro and each time the eye did not hit.

So we thank you Lord God for Cyclone Steve with its power and its wind and rain.
Its gone past now, it had to leave. Things could have been worse but we were saved.
Praise you God for hearing our prayers. The Land now has been blessed. It has been blessed with much needed rain, to regenerate the pastures and flowers.

Good will come out of all this confusion now.
Your ways are different Oh Lord to ours.
Although Nature is awesome, to you it must bow.
Thank you for keeping us safe in your hand.

*****

How

How do the Clouds stay up in the Sky?
How does a Baby learn to Cry?
How does a Bird begin to Fly?
How do we see with our Naked Eye?
How do we Talk?
How do we Sing?
How do we Love?
How do we Swim?
How do we Laugh?
How do we Sigh?
How do we Praise our God on High?
How do we Think?
How do we Drink?
How do we Walk?
How do we Remember?
How do we Play?
These are most things that we can do.

But -
How do the Clouds stay up in the sky?
How does the Wind Blow?
How do we know all that we Know?

*****

Jessie 1st. August 2023.

I am CARNARVON.

I am CARNARVON don't you see?
Why not come and visit me?
I have Sandy Beaches you could only dream about
and you may see my marvellous Water Spouts.
They are the Blowholes on the Ocean side, where
Fish and Turtles, also Whales reside. Sunsets are
glorious here you know, CARNARVON is
somewhere you need to go.
You could sample one of our fresh fish dinners, they
really are all great winners.
We have Hotels, Motels and Caravan Parks, a Jetty
only to look at - as it is falling apart.
The Museum is here, visit and see the History of Old
Times. Rusty Train Engines to delight some of your
soul ties. We even have a special Space Tracking
Station. The tour relives the Pride of our Nation.

I am CARNARVON don't you see?
Hopefully you may like to visit me!
Watch the incredible Sunsets, Swim in the Ocean.
Visit Banana & Vegie Plantations, along our Dry
River Bed. Oh! what more could you ask of me?
Sunshine each new day is Free. Some people visit
then decide to stay and others just leave and go away.
Many wish they could come back - but circumstances
do not allow. Memories can last a lifetime though.
A Carnarvon visit could be a memory to treasure.

I am CARNARVON where the Desert meets the Sea.

*****

Jessie. Friday 5th. June 2020.

Is it there or is it there?

Is it here or is it there, let me see - is it anywhere?
It must be somewhere because I used it.
I was holding on and walking with it.
Now here I am and here I sit, trying to make sense of it.
I try to think and think again and moan and grown saying what a pain, to waste my time looking and looking walking from room to room.
It must be hiding somewhere and I have to find it soon.
Yes it is my Walking Stick - trying to hide from me again.
But it can't go far on it's one leg because it needs me to move it.
When I find it, I shall hold it's handle -
to walk with me until it hides it's self again!

*****

4th. August 2024. Sunday.

Lunch Time

It's nearly lunch time now and what have I done?
Nothing much it seems under the Sun.
But I did get up and not stay in bed.
Mainly because this body needs to be fed.
So up I got to start off the day, to get washed and dressed.
We must get that out of the way, before we think of Breakfast.
Now what shall it be?
Something cooked or something on toast?
Maybe some fruit or cereal as well as the toast?
    Goodness me the time has flown!
    Never mind now.
    It will be Lunch time soon..

*****

Jessie. 8th. June 2024.

My Trimmed tree.

My Tree that was trimmed.
It is now sprouting new branches.
Little twigs and new leaves.
Beautiful and strong are the new shoots now.
They are coming from the old worn branches on the trunk of the tree.
So lovely, fresh and green is the new growth.
Later on there will be flowers, they will be red, bright red a conical shape.
Full of nectar for the birds to fly onto and drink the nectar.
There will be little green feathered birds who will alight so gently on the branches, or hover near the flowers to drink in the nectar.
What a marvelous thing the tree is, standing stout and strong.
      A blessing for us to behold.

*****

Jessie. 20th. May 2024. Monday.

Power Pole.

8am . The Power went off !!!
Four or more Electricians were out the front of our house, to replace the Electric Power Pole.
Two large crane like equipment's were there, plus various vehicles etc.,
They had to remove the overhead wires, before lifting the very tall Power Pole out of the ground to lower it down to ground level.
Then erect the new Pole and join up all the wires to it.
It's taken four hours so far and they are still working on it.
I was able to boil a saucepan on our Gas Stove to make a Cuppa.
What a blessing on a cold morning to have something warm to drink.
So no computer work till the Power comes back on.
A chance to catch up on other things that needed to be done!

*****

Jessie.   August 2024.

Rain

Have you heard the sound of the rain?
It came today with a gentle drizzle, then a bit faster
with a Pita Patter sounding on the ground.
Suddenly the Heavens opened and the rain came down
so fast, it came to flood the pathways and to water the
parched land of our North Western Australia.
The Gascoyne area of Sheep Stations and
Plantations would welcome the recent rain.
So that there could be grain for the Sheep and
Cattle to eat.
Produce would flourish for Fruit and Vegies.
Rain is a life line for us to share, to fill our rivers and
Streams everywhere.
I made a video to capture the sound -
          The Sound of the falling rain.
It's nice to treasure the refreshing sound of the rain
coming down from the overcast sky.
Cooling our land in the Winter from the fierce heat of
the hot summer Sun.
So let us be glad for the rain that we need to grow
the plants that sprout from the seeds.
Tropical Rain Forests rely on the rain, also tall trees,
the birds and the Bees that collect the nectar produced
from the flowers.
Let's be grateful for Sunshine and Rain that comes
on our Planet to Revive and Sustain.

*****

Jessie. 18th. July 2024. Thursday.

So very Dear.

My dearest love you have died.
So far I really haven't cried.
The grief is so deep, it's difficult to sleep.
How can I accept this fact.
For now I put on an act, so that others don't
know that I really loved you so.
I know you loved me, our love was meant to
be. I didn't get to say goodbye. Now I feel I live
a lie.
Never to hold or touch the one I loved so much.
Your eyes used to shine as they met with mine.
To be held in your embrace, to touch your dear
face.
I remember for ever our cheeks pressed
together.
For-ever our love was meant to be.
Your dear face now I'll never see.
But memories never die. Our love was not a lie.
     If only you were here.
     You were so very dear.

******

The Branch

The Branch looked dead, as dead as could be.
But suddenly, suddenly there was me.
I sprouted out from the dead looking Branch.
So gently I came forth on a little stalk.
Then surprise, surprise, I started to move about.
And I had a little tiny sprout of green.
The prettiest green you have ever seen.
Now I have grown into a leaf.
So soft and beautiful to touch and feel.
Also I have Brothers and Sisters all around.
They have sprouted from the other dead looking branches.
The wind is now blowing and we are waving about.
What a glorious picture our tree is alive.
Alive with green leaves now what is this?
Little buds are coming upon our stalks.
They are opening up as lovely Red Blooms.
Oh! What a picture to behold.
The tree has risen from being near dead and now is alive to live once more.
New Branches can give shade to the earth with Nectar from the Flowers for the Birds and bees.
Nature is Wonderful for all to see.

Especially for me as a New Green Leaf !

*****

Jessie Sunday 28th. April 2024

The Wind is Blowing.

The Wind is blowing the leaves are flying.
It is so gusty the Wind today.
Let us watch as it blows things away.
To stand in the midst of the Wind is great, to feel it move around your body. Also to blow through your hair.
Where did it come from?
Where does it go to?
We can never know.
Listen to the Wind in the trees.
The trees seem to love it as they sway back and forth with their branches.
You cannot touch the Wind but you can feel it when it blows against your body.
Sometimes it can try to blow you along.
Then other times it is just a gentle Breeze.
I love to hear the rustle of the leaves in the trees.
To watch them move back and forth like dancing to the Wind.

*****

Jessie. 21st. January 2023.

We Can

We are in this world of sin.
We do not have to take part in it.
We have been given a conscience.
We can choose to do right or to sin.
We can do all lovely things
We can sing and dance
We can eat and drink
We can love or not love
We can swim or drown
We can walk or run
We can write or draw
We can choose what we want
We can help others or not help
We can do all these things
We can do so much in this world
We can do good things instead of bad
We can decide not to sin
We can use our brain to decide
We can use our heart to discern
We can love The Lord our God
We can love each other
We can therefore have no need to sin.

*****

Jessie. 15th. March 2017.

Letter to a Friend....(Elephants on the Roof!)

Well I haven't written to you for a while so just had to tell you this, thought it may cheer you up but then it may not but never mind eh! I am writing anyway.

What I was going to tell you was, that during a phone conversation 9am with my Daughter who lives over 1,000klms away, (you know the one) I said to her "wait a minute, what's that noise?" She said she could not hear any noise (it sort of didn't go through the phone, I never thought of that at the time), so I said "Oh! It's alright it's the Wheelie Bin coming up the drive, so I know my friend Joan has arrived" Then when my Daughter could speak through her laughter she said, "well now, my friends arrive in a car!

Maybe it's different where you live, how on earth does she get into it? It makes you wonder why my family love to take the 'Mickey' out of me when I say things sometimes in a different way to them? If you don't know what 'taking the Mickey' means - well, it means to make fun out of what someone says. I must say that we have some quite interesting conversations over the airways, meaning the phone of course.

My friend Joan had been pulling the Wheelie Bin up the driveway as it had just been emptied prior to her arrival. Our garbage collection comes early Tuesday mornings along this road, so we put our Wheelie Bin out the night before, otherwise if it is not out there when the Garbage Disposal Truck arrives we have to keep it till the next week! It is quite interesting to see all the Wheelie Bins in a row at the end of each persons driveway. Some hanging over with rubbish, others neat and clean. When my friend Joan came through the Studio door - minus Wheelie Bin of course, we both agreed that the day was Tuesday - things usually happen on our Tuesday mornings - Social and clear up days.

Joan comes to give me a hand but we spend the first part of that time to catch up on things with a Cuppa, which I make in the Microwave, then I have my breakfast while we catch up on the previous weeks events

I was able to tell Joan that earlier in the morning I was woken up about 6am with what sounded like a herd of Elephants on the roof, right above my head. After laying there for five to ten minutes mainly in shock thinking the roof was coming in, I got up to see what was going on. Well it was just getting daylight and sprinkling with rain outside. However, I was very brave, went out through the back door in my dressing gown plus hair curlers to look up at the roof, quite fearful of what I was going to see, well there was nothing there! So, came back and went out the front door, hoping of course that no one was walking by to see me in my cozy red dressing gown and hair curlers. It was still sprinkling with rain, I looked up at the front roof - nothing!

Well to cut a long story short, I came in and had a think about it. Then light dawned in my brain as I thought back to the previous day when my Son went up on the roof to take the rest of the plastic bags and elastic bands off of the end Whirly Gig. It had been tied up for about three years to stop it whirling around as we thought it may have been causing part of the leak when it rained, coming through the Studio ceiling. Over the last year I kept finding odd pieces of plastic on the ground, in the garden and driveway, then realized that the plastic bag had been disintegrating due to our hot sun over the years. So the day before the noise on the roof, my Son undid the plastic bag and elastic bands from the Whirligig which then caused it to begin Whirling around. What happened was, the poor thing couldn't quite make it going round and round, so it was stopping, starting and grating on it's bearings with the terrible shuddering noise emanating through the house.

After another call to my Son he went up and fixed it, wrapping it up in rubber bands to make it immobile, that means that it cannot Whirl again (no plastic bags this time). Not sure whether to get a new one or not, Whirligig that is, I will have to think about that! Looks an odd sight sitting on top of the roof wrapped in black Rubber Bands. But never mind, this is our world and possibly no one will notice it! Most people don't look up at other peoples roof tops, it's surprising what some roof's have on them.

The other Whirligig on our roof has been working very well except that time when the wind blew a twig into it's whirly bits and kept jarring it, till the twig twanged out. It is handy to have someone who can get up on the roof sometimes because us Senior Citizens I am told should not get up there. (I wonder why)?!

Monday evening the night before all this went on I was taking an armful of Newspapers out through the back door not able to see where I was putting my feet of course and stood on something very, very soft, then came the terrible scream. I was standing on Harry - as I took my foot off of him, the next foot trod on him - poor thing. (It does shake you up a bit when you stand un-expectantly on your pet). You may remember him, he is our boy cat, anyway he went off to lick his wounds, thank goodness he received no lasting damage and seems to have forgiven me -

I suppose he has to forgive as I am the one who feeds him.

You can see it's not always easy being a Senior Citizen with all the new technology that we have to learn and all the things we have to cope with, including Whirligigs on the roof, garbage collections, looking after pets, trying not to stand on their paws. Do you know that our electric alarm clock went off three times during the night a few nights ago and I hadn't even set it. After the third time that it had woken me, I was up once again with the torch, looking for my glasses to see how to turn it off.   Cont'd....

No wonder some of us wake up a bit tired with Elephants on the roof and Alarm clocks going off un-expectantly.

I think I had better close, Oh, before I go, must say that I don't have any of those Senior Moments anymore (you know when you can't remember things) I have decided to have Intellectual Interludes sounds, much better and we needn't then be classed as Seniors, because Intellectual Interludes can operate at any age.

Am glad I have written this to you before I forget what I was going to write.

Hope to hear from you one of these days if you remember who I am.

Just incase you have forgotten - I am your friend Jessie.

Hope you have a good day today.

Love Jessie. (that's me)

Beware of a Comfortable Toilet Seat

I phoned my Sister in another Country, she said the other day she had fallen off her special toilet seat, which was on the toilet and it had fallen on top of her, wedging her between the toilet and the bath. Laying there with her knickers around her ankles she couldn't get up so she said some ....naughty words, while trying to get the Senior seat off of her body.

Laying there, remembered her Husband was having breakfast at the table in the kitchen while reading the Newspaper.

So decided to call out 'help, help' no answer came. After calling and shouting for some time, her husband who didn't hear her, wondered why she was so long in the bathroom. He went and knocked gently on the door, saying "Honey are you alright in there"? 'No' she shouted "Open the .... door" - he didn't hear her. He knocked a bit louder and said "are you alright, shall I open the door"?

"Open the .....door I can't get up" she said.

Well, what a sight beheld his eyes when he opened the door. His half naked elderly wife laying on the floor, with the large toilet seat on top of her, wedged on the floor near the bath.

"Can I help you up Honey?" he asked.

"Just get this seat of me" she shouted.

Being quite deaf he did not hear what she said, so walking in holding on to his walking stick he tried to pull her up. Looking up at him she said "pull your short P.J's up your Crown Jewels are falling out" ..... What a sight this must have been.!

Well he took the seat off of her and helped pull her up.
So with no knickers on, he helped her into the breakfast room to recover. Also he could not balance very well without his walking stick which he had left in the Bathroom.!
My Sister was a prominent person in her town, very particular and would have been so embarrassed to have her husband see her like that.
I laughed so much as she told me this over the phone, it was priceless to envisage .

A Tree

Will you come and look at me, touch me and feel me
- I am a tree.
I am tall and strong with a beautiful Trunk.
My Branches are like arms that spread out and reach to the sky.
I love to feel the Breeze on my Leaves as they gently blow and wave about.
But when the gusty wind does blow, my Branches move with the force of the strong wind.
Some times I am blessed with Blossom and flowers.
Then I look so pretty, hoping that you would notice me.
If only you could give me a Hug that would be so special to me.
Remember that I am only a tree but I do have feelings you see.
So love me and Hug me if you can, let me feel your heart beat just for a moment, making us one.

*****

Jessie. 27th. October. Sunday 2024.

My painting of a Wind Blown Tree near Geraldton.
N.W. Australia.

I took your Hand

I took your hand when your were small, so tiny you were back then.
But then you started to grow and I tried to show you the way to go.
Each phase of your life I have held your hand, not wanting to let you go.
But your life was for you to lead so I could not hold you back.
But in my heart and in my mind I could still hold your precious hand.
However its now your turn to hold my hand.
As I have grown old and frail.
But I still remember your little hand in mine.
When you were my lovely child.

*****

Jessie. 22nd. March 2025. Saturday.

A GRAPE

Have you ever thought about me hanging on the Vine?
I am a Grape you know and taste just Divine.
Us Grapes hang in Clusters.
Many hang there together as we gradually grow.
Lots of colours we are on different Vines.
Red, Green, Purple and White, some even Black.
Each colour has a different name.
Some can be Seedless and very sweet.
Many of us are made into Juice, some juice is frozen for special treats.
But it makes us squishy and makes us squirm, when we are made into a delicious Jam.
However, one of our best transitions is that we can be made into Wine.
How divine to be made into Wine that gladdens the heart and makes you smile.
Yes us Grapes are a good Medicine too.
Taste us and eat us wherever your are. ....
So I am a Grape, hanging on a Vine.
The Earth and the Sun helps us to grow.
Then my Bunch grows down to make a nice Cluster, with other Bunches that are on the same Vine.
Just hanging there waiting for Harvest time.
Then you can make of us, what you will.
Maybe just eat as a beautiful fruit off the Vine or make a delicious lovely wine. !
    What ever you do we are here just for you.

*****

Jessie. 29th. October 2024. Tuesday.

Pen/Ink Drawing - Roses.

Just Sitting

So I am here, not here or there, just sitting
outside taking in the air.
The Sun is warm and lovely, the Breeze is gentle
just now.
A little Bird flies past fast and some Butterflies
flap their wings as they fly along on the Breeze.
My plants look lovely as some now have their
Blossoms.
An Aloe Vera plant has its flowers quite high on its
stalk.
Most of my Plants are lovely greens, Cactus Plants
that thrive here in the hot sun.
I have trees all around to give really good shade.
Pot Plants adorn our Patio, where I can sit and
contemplate the day.
Here I can count my Blessings One by One.
What a lovely way to spend a bit of time.
Just to sit and think or dream of all the things that
could have been and all the things that are to come.
So come with me and sit and think.
Come away for a while from the Kitchen Sink.
The chores will still be there for you to do.
Maybe take a bit of time in the day for you.

*****

Jessie. 7th. November 2024. Thursday.

Have a lovely day Today.

Jealousy

Are you Jealous, no not me !
It's the other people who are jealous of me.
No wait a minute, have I go that wrong?
Maybe jealousy can come out in a Song.
We can be jealous of our neighbours and friends,
with what they have and we have not, a brand new house, a car a pool.
Oh! fancy being like a jealous fool.
They deserve these things, they have worked for them.
We cannot all have the same as each other.
That young Mum with a baby, so lovely to see,
why oh why was that not me?
We cannot live our lives like others, let us love our Sisters and Brothers.
We should not covet what others have, so let us be thankful for our Bread.
If we have food and shelter and friends, what more could we ask, then we need not offend.
No need to offend others with our jealous wants.
Let us show we appreciate the blessings they have.
Do we have talents and love we can share?
Then no need to be jealous of things that they have.
Turn away from all jealous thoughts and deeds.
Jealousy eats away at our hearts and minds.
It's hard sometimes that we want what others have.
If we count our blessings as we really should, then jealous thoughts will fly away.
And will leave us to have a better Day.

*****

The Linen Line

I am sitting outside watching the clothes on the
Linen Line Dancing in the Breeze.
Yes, the wind has just started to come in.
So as I looked up at a Tee Shirt it started to move about
waving its arms dancing with it's body, also moving as if
music was playing to the music of the Breeze.
It is hanging upside down on the Linen Line pegged up by
the waist band.
The Tee Shirt is next to a fine white Pillowcase which is
now waving to and fro.!
Oh! the joy they may feel flapping in the Breeze with just a
bit of Sunshine to dry them out.
This is Winter time so I can see a nice Blue Wincey full
length Nightdress, pegged up by the shoulders dancing to
the Rhythm of the Breeze.
A pair of warm Red Bed Socks pegged up by their toes
would be ready to wear again for bed, when night time
comes.
Lots of other things are hanging there, a towel, plus some
tea towels, next to a Bra, and fleecy white trousers, also
underwear, pants (knickers) and a long warm scarf.
That's it - I think as I sit here with my feet up on our Patio
settee. The Linen Line has a shade cloth cover over the top
to keep the hot sun off in the Summer, with Pot Plants
around the central pole.
All the clothes are dancing now in our lovely glorious
weather. There is also a Garden Ornament of a Black Tin
Dog sitting watching the movement of the washing.

Must be one of those Tranquil Halcyon days we sometimes
hear about.
*****

Jessie 11th November 2024.

Write a Poem?

Is this the day to write a Poem?
I am not sure what to write, my mind is busy and tends to roam after waking up from the night.
Today is a new day only just beginning so what shall we do today then?
After our Breakfast we have the whole morning to come and go wherever we please.
Let today be a good day to think of others, maybe our Sisters or maybe our Brothers.
Strangers may come across our path, let us greet them and maybe laugh.
Today we could have joy if we choose, sadness and grief maybe with us but we can choose to put them aside for a while. Let us look at the morning with fresh eyes.
Remember there is a whole new world outside, just waiting for us to explore.
If we can go outside we can sit and hear the birds sing and look at the sky.
Then wonder why they are always so cheerful, flitting about, being busy and always they seem to be content.
So this then is not a poem after all but it makes us think about the morn (Morning).

Now we can make a great decision of what we would like to do today!

*****

Jessie. 27th. September 2019.

* Today *

Today will never come again, so what are we going to do?
It gives us time to think for a while of what a lovely day it could be.
First let us think of our days that are past they seem to have gone so very fast.
But today we can do something different again.
Something special just for today.
Maybe phone a friend and have a chat.
This maybe our last day, fancy that.
However we may have many more days to come.
Each day will come - never to return.
Because Tomorrow will be another day to treasure.
Today will be gone and when -
Tomorrow comes it will be called Today!

*****

Jessie Saturday 30th. November 2024.

* Sing *

Sing, Sing, today. Sing a Song that you know.
Sing from your heart, that is the best way to start.
Sing out loud, Sing so softly. Maybe make up a song as you Sing.
Old songs from your memory can be a joy to Sing.
Even remember them from your childhood.
Maybe a Lullaby will come to mind.
Remember - that can be a different kind.
Sing out loud, let our voice be heard.
Maybe listen to the song of a Bird.
Sing outside, Sing indoors.
Sing in the Shower behind closed doors.
What does it matter then?
Let your Song be Sung in the morning or evening, maybe during the day, or when ever you feel a Song coming on!

*****

Jessie. Friday 20th. December 2024.

Beauty

Beauty is not just in the beholder,
(that is the one that is looking at you).
Let them know that beauty is within you.
Tell yourself that beauty is loveliness.
Beauty then shows on your face, if you have peace in your heart.
You may not be good looking, intelligent or smart.
But beauty can be on your face by the look of contentment that is in your heart.
Superficial beauty of makeup on the face or the body will be gone.
But the beauty of grace, contentment and peace, can be everlasting in your soul, in your heart, in your being, in your understanding.
Yes beauty is fleeting but love in your heart can flow out to others if only you can let it flow to bless others that come before you each day.
Let them know that you care for them talk to them, help them.
Then beauty will shine from you and it will not be fleeting.

*****

Jessie. Thursday 19th. April 2018

M.U. Christmas Lunch

There we were ariving for our Christmas Lunch,
summoned to be on time at Annie's house.
It took a while for everyone to arrive by car or on
Shanks's pony (that means she walked) from a few
houses away.
One with a walking frame on wheels, one with a
child.
Bearing gifts all wrapped up to share as surprises,
to choose from after lunch.
Yes it was a Bring and Share lunch.
Oh! the variety, Yummy Sandwiches with mysterious
fillings, presented beautifully on several platters.
Spicy Dips with crudities, Cakes - Sponge Cake,
Lamington's with Cream fillings, Rum Balls and
Marshmallows.
Best Bone China, too precious really to handle for us
M.U.'s but was beautiful.
Then the horror of horror's, ones hand knocked over
a cup full of hot Tea.
Amazing how far it spilt - over the table cloth.
Over one members trousers - but not even a chip or a
dent on the beautiful cup and saucer, thank goodness!
Conversation was typical at our get together's around
the lunch table, with most M.U.'s talking at once
while also eating and drinking.
Two with hearing aids, one not able to see very well
and a visitor who thought we were all really not quite
with it!

Cont'd......

However - it was most enjoyable, with one recovering from double knee surgery, one almost deaf, one diagnosed as sight impaired, also one whose tooth had fallen out from one of her front teeth that morning.
You may well laugh but remember four ladies in their eighties, mixing with the not so young members it was really special.
A typical M.U. meeting.

Choosing a Gift, we took it in turns, admiring whatever each one found lurking in the Christmas wrapping.
Then we were to pray at home for the one that received our anonymous gift.

*****

Praise The Lord for our M.U. Carnarvon Group.

Tuesday.. 20th. November 2018 Jessie.

I want to write a Poem

I want to write a Poem, yes I really do.
But what can I write?
The morning is here so I need not fear.
I have all the day to write and say, whatever is in my heart to make that great start.
To begin to write a Poem is a wonderful thing.
So here we are then what shall I say?
Should I let it rest in my heart till the next day?
I have made a start.
Just to write, is enabling my thoughts to go on to write something Special.
         - Someday soon -

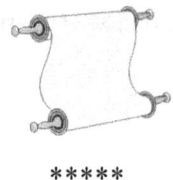

*****

Jessie. 24th. September 2021

The Tray
I am a Tray - Do you like Trays?

We are Trays...... I am a very Classy one with beautiful printed Roses on and a wooden frame around, I have a soft pad underneath to rest on your knees. I am very useful to use for writing cards or letters while sitting comfortably in your favourite chair. I was a Birthday Present for my owner.
***

This one that I am is metal, all carved with roses and handles on two sides, with a metal rose motif on each handle. I am a Circular Tray. My owner brought me back from her visit to America. I am very special, made from a soft grey looking metal.
***

Next one - has a cushion underneath I am a nice cream colour plastic, with inserts around to use as a Craft Tray, to put pencils in etc; while working the on the flat surface.
***

My Tray is a useful Tray to put a Laptop on. I too have a cushion underneath. I have a small movable over tray light, plus a hole to put a Cuppa or something in.
***

So, I am an Oval Silver Tray to use for guests while they eat dinner on their laps for the evening meal, to be comfortable watching television in the lounge room.
***

Now, I am the newest one that stops the plates from sliding about while people carry plates of food on me.
***

Us Trays are very useful, everyone seems to take us for granted not realizing how useful we are to carry things or to use for so many different activities. Please wash me and keep me clean, because I like holding things for you. It makes me happy that I can be of Service in a Posh house, or a Poor home, a Castle or a Café. I look forward to you holding me.!

- I think I am Special -

*****

Jessie...... December.......2024.

Speak from the Heart.

Out of the heart, the mouth speaks.
What is in our heart today?
Is it love, peace, joy, or misery and regret?
Let our heart see the things that are good.
Don't dwell on the bad.
Misery and strife may be all around us.
But we need to choose!
Yes, we have a choice to look past the sad things in our life and live in the new day that is ours today.
So start to speak out words of goodness and grace.
Talk to each other of nice things today and sadness and sorrow will begin to go away.
Let us speak from our mouth.
 - good things -
From our heart.

*****

Wonderful Day!

Oh! What a Wonderful Day!
The Sky is Blue, what a beautiful Hue.
A Bird is Chirping, a leaf is blowing in the Breeze.
The sun is warm today.
The thinnest Branches on our trees begin to sway, as if they are listening to music.
The music of the Universe.
Can you hear the breeze?
Close your eyes to see and hear the sounds of the world around us.
Beautiful Day.
Wonderful Day.
One to treasure if only for a few moments.

*****

Jessie. Saturday 4th. January 2025.

My Homeland.

Australia is my homeland now far away from across the sea.
This is the place I need to be with beautiful oceans and sandy beaches that stretch as far as the eye can see.
Softest sand and warm, warm waters!
Sub tropical land is where I live now, with Palm Trees around so big and grand.
Different Birds with Parrots abound, sometimes squawking and making a noise.
They have colourful and beautiful Feathers.
Wildlife is here in this Sunburnt land.
All are different Creature's from the Country that I came from - Creepy, Crawlies, Goannas and Crocodiles that we had not seen back home.
This has been my home now for many years.
I could write pages and pages of what it is like.
But just for now will say - Good night.

*****

Jessie. 18th. January 2025.

Remember Me?

I sit and wait for you to come
but now you are interested in number one.
So I sit and wait and you do not come.
Then I wonder will this day be the one?
I have lots of things to do today
what they are I cannot say.
But I could put them all aside
if you could open the door wide.
Then I would see your lovely smile
and we could talk just for a while.
What a lovely day that would be
when you decide to visit me.
Sadness and loneliness would go away
when you visit me for the day.
Just for a while is all I ask.
Before the days have all gone past.

*****

19th. April 2025. Jessie. Saturday.
Written for all those dear soles who sit and wait!

Can you see the Wind?

There is a wind out on the horizon too far for the eye to see. There's a wind out on the horizon too far, far, far away to see.
How can you see the wind? How can you see the breeze? The wind moves fast, faster and faster.
The breeze is gentle, so soft and free.
Look at the leaves on the nearest tree.
Rustling in the breeze, they move so gently, they move about so lovely to see.
You cannot see the breeze itself, it is invisible.
The leaves move. They cannot move - unless they are touched. They are touched by the unseen hand of the breeze. The wind blows faster than a breeze, it can become so strong. Wind can become a mighty gale, a tornado, a whirlwind, a willy-willy - tall and strong, reaching to the sky!
Try standing in a gale force wind it moves you along. Face it and you cannot move forward very fast, it tries to push you back. Where does it come from? You cannot see but Oh! you can feel the force in a gale. There is no slack, until it suddenly stops and is spent, is gone, is finished.
Wait, - where did it go then this mighty wind?
No-one really knows. It seems to have it's own mind.
Then watch out - because it can turn around, come back at a different angle. Do you realize the wind can whistle? Yes, it has a voice, it can sing through the trees, whistle through their branches.
Even in the towns and cities you can hear it's voice.

cont'd......

When I was a child lying in bed I used to lay and listen to the wind. It used to come whistling between the roof tops of the old houses, moving around the chimney pots. It would sometimes whistle so loud, people would fear, put their heads under the covers, then wait for it to go past. But I loved listening to the wind. It would whistle and blow with great whirring and wooing sounds, as it wove it's way between the chimneys. Still - none of us can see it, it has no colour, it has no form, it is invisible to our eyes. Excepting we can see the movement in the things it touches. Like the finger of God moving over the earth, it ceases not day nor night. Sometimes it's a curse, sometimes a blessing. What would we do here in the heat of the day, if no breeze came off the ocean? In Summer we wait for the breeze to come just after lunchtime. We look and wait! Then if it is late we complain, because we wait for the cooling breeze. If it comes from inland - it's a hot breeze, then we long for it to go away. During Winter it's a cold wind that comes. We can feel the wind in different ways, hot, cool, strong, weak, gentle. The wind has substance but still the eye cannot see it! It is invisible but is forever present somewhere on our Planet. Have you watched it move the clouds, sometimes fast, sometimes slow.
The beautiful patterns are created by the wind.
Look at the clouds, the sky at Sunset, the Masters Hand using the wind as a paintbrush.
Could we ever accomplish such Art? Never!
What a wonder to look and see the clouds and the sky.
Cont'd......

If the wind ceased it would be so sad.
There would be no lovely pictures in the sky.
The great formations changing and changing,
the colours of the Sunset rearranging, minute by
minute until the Sun goes down.
Then the pictures are gone.
But wait - The wind has not gone!
It's still here moving around us everywhere.
Can you see it? No!
Look and see, walk on the Beach, walk on the grass,
feel the wind on your face.
The flowers move with grace. Waves on the ocean
move with the wind.
Where is it now is it here, is it there?
Feel it on your face, sometimes it's gentle.
The wind is free.
It's here for you and it's here for me.
Come out of your shelter, come out of your house.
Come out in the wind, brace yourself, go for a walk
or stand still for a moment, share in the breeze, stand
under a tree, touch it's leaves.
The wind hasn't time to stand still for long.
It goes with a whistle, it goes with a song,
Oh! to be free as a breeze today.
Wind, wind, what do you say as you move over
the earth and you make things sway.
No-one can capture you, you are so free.
Wind, wind, you can touch all that you see.

      Come Wind, come touch me.

*****

Sleeping Hibiscus

A Petal fell and lay on the ground.
Beautiful dark red colour, so soft so lovely.
But no, it was not just a Petal it was the whole flower.
Because it was a Sleeping Hibiscus which only opens halfway.
So laying on the ground, from a distance, looked just like a Petal.
This year the small tree was full of blossoms.
Friends wonder and hope to see them open up.
But they only open halfway and that is the most that they do.
However the tree looks incredible with all the Blooms showing off their lovely deep Crimson/Red Flowers and pretty green foliage.
   What a privilege for us to see!

*****

3rd. June 2023.

Sky

At the moment all Grey Sky with a White Bird
Flying across. The white so white and the grey so
grey. Yes this is truly a Wintry day.
The rain has ceased we had only a shower.
Everything smells so fresh, the shower finished just
under the hour. Things look brighter here after the
rain. Maye later on it will rain again!
The flowers look pretty so and fresh and clean.
The grass smells like new and the trees look so green.

Here in the North it's mostly heat and dust. So when
the rain comes, - to go out and look is a must. Well I
can see through our doorway that the sky is still grey.
The morning has gone now so maybe this sky is here
for the day! It seems most strange to look out and see
not a speck of blue sky where it should be. But somewhere under the darkness of grey our blue sky is waiting with white fluffy clouds.

The mantle of grey is dreary, so dull. But the rain is so
precious we need our Dams full. The Pastures, the
Plains will then grow again once more, to feed all the
animals who are hungry and sore.
They are sore from the heat and the dust and the flies.
They will relish this rain now, God's gift from the
skies. Another white bird flew over just then.
Now it's gone and the rain has just started again.

*****

Jessie. .... 1994.

The War is over.

The war is over now what can we do?
It's a new day dawning for me and you.
The Sky is blue and the Sun is shining, so no more crying and no more whining.
Life is to be lived, like we should.
Lets get up and go, so we really could dance and sing, talk to our friends as our New day hopefully never ends.
We survived the war, we are alive!
With food to eat, we can now survive.
What a pretty picture the garden makes, no fear now, we can sit by the lakes.
The war is over we are set free.
It is really wonderful we all agree, no looking over our shoulder as we each grow older, with peace in our hearts and a great new start.

*****

Pages Numbers.

As there is no Index, I will leave this page blank for you to write the Page Number and Title that you may like to read again. To save you hunting through the book. I do hope you have enjoyed some of the writings and Illustrations.
Thank you. Jessie.

This Page is for you to write your own small Poem, if you would like to.

My Pen/Ink Drawing of the old One Mile Jetty that we had in Carnarvon before the ravages of time and most recent Cyclone.

The Old Bridge in Carnarvon over the River Gascoyne.

An Oil Painting by the Author.